MW01674745

CITIZEN OF THE KINGDOM

LIVING UNDER GOD'S RULE

PRESENTED TO

BY

DATE

Lifeway Press®
Brentwood, Tennessee

ISBN 978-1-0877-8489-2
Item 005842361
Dewey Decimal Classification Number: 242
Subject Heading: DEVOTIONAL LITERATURE / BIBLE STUDY AND TEACHING / GOD

Printed in the United States of America.

Student Ministry Publishing
Lifeway Resources
200 Powell Place, Suite 100
Brentwood, Tennessee 37027

We believe that the Bible has God for its author; salvation for its end; truth, without any mixture of error, for its matter; and that all Scripture is totally true and trustworthy. To review Lifeway's doctrinal guideline, please visit https://www.lifeway.com/about/doctrinal-guidelines.

publishing team

Director, Next Gen Publishing
Chuck Peters

Manager, Small Group Resources
Karen Daniel

Writer
Mike Lovato

Content Editor
Kyle Wiltshire

Production Editor
April-Lyn Caouette

Graphic Designer
Shiloh Stufflebeam

TABLE OF CONTENTS

04
intro

05
getting started

06
seek first His kingdom

40
Your kingdom come

74
how to live as strangers and exiles

108
right, wrong, or illegal?

INTRO

One of the greatest blessings we have in our lives today is our country. It's not perfect, and there certainly are dark times in our history. Even today, there are bitter fractures and divides among the people who live here. But the freedoms we are afforded and the opportunities we have to achieve our dreams are reasons why it's such a great country—flaws and all.

For many, having a national identity provides a sense of belonging. Belonging and feeling connected to a group is important for everyone. So is having an identity. We strive passionately to create both of these things for ourselves, and for many of us, belonging and identity are wrapped up in the place we live, the place we come from, or the place we call home.

For followers of Jesus, we have belonging and identity, but they are not rooted in our nation. This wonderful country is not our true home; it's not where we place our ultimate allegiance. If you are a follower of Jesus, your ultimate allegiance belongs to Him. You are a citizen of another kingdom: not a kingdom of this world but a kingdom that is to come—the kingdom of God.

So, what do we do until His kingdom has fully arrived here on earth? For now, while we still physically live in this country, we must have an understanding of our true citizenship and a guide to help us navigate the here and now. That's what this book is all about. God commands us to be good citizens of the world and the country we live in, but He also demands our deepest loyalties. We are citizens of His kingdom above any other citizenship we might possess.

GETTING STARTED

This devotional contains thirty days of content, broken down into sections. Each day is divided into three elements—**discover**, **delight**, and **display**—to help you grow in your faith.

DISCOVER

This section helps you examine the passage in light of who God is and determine what it says about your identity in relationship to Him. Included here is the daily Scripture reading and key verses, along with illustrations and commentary to guide you as you learn more about God's Word.

DELIGHT

In this section, you'll be challenged by questions and activities that help you see how God is alive and active in every detail of His Word and your life.

DISPLAY

Here's where you take action. This section calls you to apply what you've learned through each day.

Each day also includes a prayer activity at the conclusion of the devotion.

Throughout the devotional, you'll also find extra items to help you connect with the topic personally, such as Scripture memory verses and interactive articles.

SECTION 1

SEEK FIR
HIS
KINGDO

We don't think of our country as a kingdom, but everyone has a king. That king is the person or thing to which we give our highest affections. As followers of Jesus, our desire should be to honor Him as our King and to seek His kingdom above all other people or things.

DAY 1

HIS KINGDOM FIRST

READ MATTHEW 6:25-34.

"But seek first the kingdom of God and his righteousness, and all these things will be provided for you." — Matthew 6:33

DISCOVER

You're growing up in a world that can be a very scary place at times. In the last few years, our country has experienced deep division, violence, financial concerns, a global pandemic, and more. These aren't just things that adults are affected by—the reality is that you probably are concerned about some of them too. As Jesus reminded His first followers and reminds us today from the pages of Scripture, our focus can't be on the worrisome things in life. Our focus has to be on His kingdom first.

The kingdom of God is all about God reigning and ruling in His creation. We seek His kingdom first when we choose to align our lives with what God says is important rather than what is naturally important to us. Jesus calls us as His followers to orient our entire lives around Him—that's what it means to seek His kingdom first.

The answers to your concerns about our country's problems aren't ever going to be solved by worrying about them or obsessing over coming up with solutions. The only hope for our country is for God's followers to seek His kingdom first instead of putting all these other things ahead of Him. The result of this focus is that God takes care of all the other parts of our lives that are a concern to us.

DELIGHT

What are some things people seek first instead of God's kingdom?

Why does Jesus tell us not to worry in this passage?

What does it mean to "seek first the kingdom of God and His righteousness" (v. 33)? What does that look like in your everyday life?

DISPLAY

Seeking God's kingdom first may sound like a huge task, but it actually starts with small steps every single day. Take a few minutes and make a list of three to five different activities you plan to spend time on during the coming week. Look at each item you've listed and evaluate whether it is focused more on God's kingdom or your own priorities. This doesn't mean you have to automatically eliminate any activity that's focused more on your own priorities. Instead, look at the items that are less focused on God, and come up with one way you can focus that activity a bit more on His kingdom.

As you close your time today in prayer, ask God to show you any areas in your life where you have worries. Commit each of those worries to God as they come to mind. Commit to seeking God's kingdom first and looking for small opportunities to come your way that allow you to be more focused on His kingdom.

DAY 2

No Other Gods

READ EXODUS 20:1-6.

Do not have other gods besides me.
— Exodus 20:3

DISCOVER

God gave the Ten Commandments to the people of Israel through Moses. As Moses stood on Mount Sinai in the Lord's presence, you have to imagine he felt overwhelmed—not only by God's presence but also by the rules God gave for His people to live by. They were simply stated yet profound in impact, challenging to keep yet necessary to honor God and others. The first four of the Ten Commandments deal with how we relate to God; the remaining six deal with how we relate to one another.

The very first commandment God gave to Moses was for His people to not have any other gods before Him. You might find yourself skimming over that first commandment a little too quickly because it may not seem to be very relevant to your life in the twenty-first century. Most of us don't bow down to gods like Baal as they did in the days of the Bible. But if you stop and think for a minute about what a false god was back then, it may help you see what a false god could be now.

A false god is anything other than God that people depend on, put their trust in, and worship. In Moses's time, this might have been a divine being who they thought was responsible for bringing the rain for crops or blessing couples with children. In our time, we may find ourselves depending on things like grades, money, romantic relationships, or even our country. But God's command to us today is the same as it was to the Israelites: we are to have no gods other than Him.

DELIGHT

What truths does God reveal about Himself in verse 2?

What are some false gods people put before God today?

Why does God take the worship of other gods so seriously?

DISPLAY

It's a good thing to be proud of our country and to celebrate the freedoms we have. But it's also possible to take our love of country to a level where it becomes more important to us than God Himself. At that point, our country has become an idol. The key is keeping things in proper perspective.

Ask yourself a hard question: Do you see yourself as an American first or as a Christian first? Both are great things, but God is calling you to put Him above anything else that would try to grab your worship and affection.

Spend some time in prayer asking God to help you keep your priorities straight when it comes to worshiping Him alone. Ask God to help you hold things in the right perspective and to not make your country into an idol. Commit yourself to seeking God above anything else in your life.

DAY 3

PRAYER PLAN

READ MATTHEW 6:5-8.

*"But when you pray, go into your private room,
shut your door, and pray to your Father who is in secret.
And your Father who sees in secret will reward you."
— Matthew 6:6*

DISCOVER

Can you imagine being in a dating relationship where you talked a big game about how much you liked the other person and how great he or she was . . . but then you never talked to that person? That probably wouldn't be a very good relationship, right? In the same way, you can't have an incredible relationship with God if you never spend time talking with Him in prayer. It's impossible to truly seek God's kingdom first without prayer.

Let's be honest, though. Prayer is a huge struggle for many of us. You might feel like you don't know what to say or what to do. Maybe you've heard someone pray with really big spiritual words and you've thought, "I could never pray like that!" Jesus gives us a simple starting place in today's verses. A healthy prayer life starts with getting yourself alone with God and not worrying about impressing other people. God wants to spend time talking with you during prayer and hearing you share your heart with Him.

DELIGHT

How does Jesus say that we are not to pray?

Why do you think prayer is a struggle for many people?

How can you focus on growing your prayer life?

DISPLAY

You probably want your life to make a difference in this world—and if you're a follower of Jesus, you probably want to make an impact for God's kingdom. We often think this impact will start through doing something "big" for God. But the very first "big" thing to do is to invest in our prayer lives. One of the benefits of finding a quiet place to pray is that it eliminates all distractions. Take a minute to list a few things that tend to distract you when you try to pray. Next to each of those items, write down a way you can try to eliminate that distraction today.

It's time to put Jesus's teaching on prayer into practice. In your prayer time today, make sure you start by finding a place to be by yourself. This can be challenging if you have siblings or pets around, but do your best! Next, allow yourself a moment to quiet all the distractions and truly be alone with God. Finally, spend time talking to God about whatever is on your mind. Ask Him to give you a deeper and more committed prayer life. Spend time both talking to God and listening to what He may be saying to you through His Word.

DAY 4

How to Find Direction

READ PSALM 119:105-112.

Your word is a lamp for my feet and a light on my path.
— Psalm 119:105

DISCOVER

Believe it or not, we haven't always been able to figure out how to get to a destination by pulling out our phones and being guided there by an app. There was a time when you had to look up directions on a desktop computer, print out the directions on paper, then bring them with you in the car. And before the internet, there was a time where you had to bring a paper map with you if you wanted to figure out where to go, or you had to get directions like "turn right at the big red barn."

The way we get around town may have changed, but God's direction for how we seek His kingdom is still the same. The primary way we know which direction to go in life is by looking to God's Word, the Bible. It's an incredible book and one of the main ways God communicates to His people. Wondering how to deal with anxiety? Dive into the Scripture for help. Confused about how to relate to other people? Look it up in the Bible. You're never going to figure out God's way of living if you try to do it on your own. You need to hear from His voice every single day, and then follow what He says.

DELIGHT

How does the author of Psalm 119 view God's Word?

How would you describe the psalmist's commitment to Scripture?

Why is the Bible so important for giving us guidance?

DISPLAY

It's easy to say you believe the Bible and follow its teachings, but does your life prove that to be true? You may not be a Bible scholar, but you can take some simple steps today to grow a deeper commitment to hearing from God through His Word. First, carve out time every day to read the Bible and reflect on what you read. It doesn't have to be hours and hours; even a few minutes a day makes a difference. Second, pick a plan to read the Bible. A resource like this one you're holding can help, or you can find some great Bible reading plans either by looking online or asking a leader at church. Third, commit to always obeying what God shows you through His Word. We show our love for God when we obey what He tells us to do.

Ask God to give you a deeper love for His Word. Ask Him to give you understanding about the parts you don't understand. Spend part of your prayer time reflecting on what you've read in Scripture today and seeking how God might want you to live it out. Make a commitment to read at least a little bit of the Bible every day.

DAY 5

THE HABIT OF WORSHIP

READ PSALM 95.

Come, let's worship and bow down; let's kneel before the LORD our Maker.
— Psalm 95:6

DISCOVER

Seeking God's kingdom means that worship is a regular habit in your life. Everybody worships something: some people worship good grades, others worship celebrities, and others worship money. Citizens of God's kingdom realize that God is to be the only object of their worship.

Psalm 95 takes us through several movements of worship. It starts in a place of joyful—even loud—celebration. Next, the psalm recognizes who God is and His role as Creator of all. The last part of the psalm moves into our response in worship, broken into two smaller pieces. The first part of that response is to put ourselves in the correct posture before God—one that recognizes that He is in control. The second part involves listening to God with the intent of obeying what He says.

Worship is about responding to God for who He is and what He has done. It's recognizing who we are in light of who He is. We are to be worshipers of God both in our times alone with Him and as we gather regularly with other followers of Jesus.

DELIGHT

What are some elements of worship that you see in Psalm 95?

How often do you see these elements of worship lived out in your personal life? How often do you see them lived out in your church?

What is the significance of the posture of worship in verse 6?

DISPLAY

We often think about worship as the time during a church service when we sing songs. Singing can absolutely be an act of worship to God, but worship is so much more than that. Think about how much greater your time worshiping with other believers on Sunday would be if you invested in personal times of worship throughout the week. Personal times of worship might include singing, but it also could have other components. You might spend time reflecting on what God has done for you. You might create a list of words that describe who God is. You can even worship God by physically changing your posture—by standing, sitting, or kneeling. Take a moment today, and during every day for the rest of this week, to carve out a personal time of worship to God. See how this changes your attitude and perspective and your worship time with other believers.

Focus your prayer time today as a time of worship. Focus first on who God is—His power, His knowledge, His glory. Praise Him specifically for aspects of each of these. Next, focus on the actions you've seen God take—sending Jesus to save you, loving you when you've been difficult to love, and ruling over the events of history and your life. Close your time by committing to a great heart of worship, both by yourself and with others.

DAY 6

A TIME FOR HUMILITY

READ 2 CHRONICLES 7:8-16.

"[If] my people, who bear my name, humble themselves,
pray and seek my face, and turn from their evil ways,
then I will hear from heaven, forgive their sin, and heal their land."
— 2 Chronicles 7:14

DISCOVER

King Solomon of Israel was given the incredible task of building a temple for the worship of God. It was an amazing building project that ended with Solomon and the people holding a time of dedication for the new temple. During this dedication, Solomon heard directly from God Himself with clear instructions for what His people were to do if tough times came their way.

These same instructions apply to us as believers today. Humble repentance is the key, and it starts in each one of us individually. When we realize that things aren't going right in our lives, verse 14 gives us a model for how we ought to approach God. We should humble ourselves, seek God's face, and turn from our sin. It's so simple that it almost seems *too* simple.

What's also key is God's promise to us. God promises to hear us, forgive us, and bring the healing we need. Yet, so often we resist putting ourselves humbly before God. We'd rather cling to our sin and pride instead of truly seeking Him.

DELIGHT

After reading today's Scripture, how would you describe the dedication and celebration of the temple?

What are the main ideas you find in the Lord's nighttime conversation with Solomon?

Why is humility sometimes such a challenge to practice?

DISPLAY

Often we want to see huge change happen for God in our communities and in our country. But the reality is that big change starts in the hearts and lives of individual followers of Jesus. Think of the instructions in verse 14 as a way we can continually live. Are you living humbly before God and others? Are you seeking God's face daily? Are you turning from sin when you're convicted of it and turning back to Jesus? Imagine how practicing these things every day could bring about supernatural change in your community and in your country.

Ask God to reveal any areas of sin that you may be hanging on to. Sometimes our sin may seem obvious to us through our actions. At other times, our sin may be lurking beneath the surface and may show up in our thought lives or inner attitudes. In either case, as God reveals sin to you, choose to humbly repent of it and seek God in a fresh way. Ask Him to empower you through the Holy Spirit to live for His glory.

MEMORY VERSE

"[IF] MY PEOPLE, WHO BEAR MY NAME,

HUMBLE THEMSELVES,

PRAY & SEEK MY FACE,

AND TURN FROM THEIR

EVIL WAYS,

then I will

HEAR FROM HEAVEN,

FORGIVE THEIR SIN,

AND HEAL THEIR LAND."

– 2 CHRONICLES 7:14

DAY 7

HIDDEN TREASURE

READ PSALM 119:6-19.

I have treasured your word in my heart so that I may not sin against you.
— Psalms 119:11

DISCOVER

Some people are great at memorizing things, and others really struggle with it. It can be tough to memorize information, whether it's multiplication facts, chemistry formulas, or even the lyrics to a song. But the value of memorization is huge. It allows us to do math quicker, pass our tests simply, or excel at vocal performances without giving it a second thought. If you're studying advanced math, can you imagine having to look up every small multiplication fact? It would take forever!

Memorizing portions of the Bible can be a huge advantage to us as Christians. We can recall verses we've memorized to help us resist temptation. Memorization brings strength and encouragement when we're feeling discouraged. It's much faster to bring verses to your mind from memory than having to go look them up every time.

Followers of Jesus who are seeking God's kingdom benefit greatly when they embrace treasuring God's Word in their hearts. God's agenda will never be far from your mind when you choose to take Scripture off the pages and into your heart by memorizing it.

DELIGHT

What are some possible ways to understand the idea of treasuring God's Word in your heart?

Why is it sometimes a struggle to memorize Scripture?

How would you describe the attitude of the psalmist towards God's Word in this passage?

DISPLAY

It probably sounds like a great idea to start memorizing Scripture. But how in the world do you actually start doing it? You can start today by coming up with a simple plan. Pick a few verses that are meaningful to you to start with. (You can even start with the verses listed in this book on pages 26–27, 60–61, and 94–95.) Take one verse at a time and repeat it to yourself over and over. You can create flash cards to help you, or use a small whiteboard and erase one word at a time. Focus on memorizing the verse accurately, even though that might seem tough. Last, but not least, always memorize the book, chapter, and verse number so you know where to direct someone if you're telling them about it.

In your prayer time, tell God about your desire (or lack of desire) to memorize Scripture. It may not feel very natural to you, so ask Him to give you the commitment to get started and to keep it going. Ask Him to show you certain verses that would be good for you to memorize and treasure in your heart.

DAY 8

WORTHY OF ALL PRAISE

READ PSALM 150.

Praise him for his powerful acts; praise him for his abundant greatness.
— Psalm 150:2

DISCOVER

Psalm 150 is a short psalm that's full of praise. Take a look—nearly every line begins with the word "praise"! This word carries with it the idea of celebration and lifting up the Lord. We worship a God who is worthy of our praise because of both His powerful acts and His abundant greatness.

God has acted powerfully throughout history. The Old Testament tells the stories of His acting on behalf of the people of Israel. His actions display a key character quality: His greatness. We worship God not just for what He has done for us but because of His very nature.

The practice of praise is incredible when we worship God through music. Psalm 150 shows us just some of the ways people at that time used music to praise God. This praise was loud, used multiple instruments, and would have been celebrated skillfully.

As you seek God's kingdom first, praise should be your attitude throughout the day. You might not always feel like praising God, but it's in those moments that you can choose to praise God, regardless of your feelings.

DELIGHT

Does the praise described in Psalm 150 look like the praise you experience regularly during worship? Why or why not?

What do you think it means to "praise God in his sanctuary" and "in his mighty expanse" (v. 1)?

How does calling "everything that breathes" (v. 6) to praise the Lord encourage you to praise Him?

DISPLAY

Fill out the chart below. In the first column, list out some of the powerful acts that God has performed. These can be acts from the Bible, from your own life, or in the lives of other people. In the second column, list ways in which God is abundantly great. These will be characteristics of who God is, such as His love, compassion, or knowledge. Hopefully you're able to list several things in each column. Circle two or three items from each column that you can praise during your prayer time this week.

GOD'S POWERFUL ACTS	GOD'S ABUNDANT GREATNESS

In your prayer time today, you're going to use the lists you created in the Display activity. Take time to praise God for the things you circled. First, praise Him for His powerful acts. Then, praise Him for His abundant greatness. As other things come to mind, focus your prayer and praise on those items as well.

DAY 9

THANKFUL WORSHIP

READ PSALM 100.

Enter his gates with thanksgiving and his courts with praise.
— Psalm 100:4

DISCOVER

We take so many things for granted in our daily lives. How often do we express our gratitude for even simple things, like having food to eat or a bed to sleep in? God calls us to approach His presence with an attitude of thanksgiving and praise. One thing thankfulness does for us is it takes the focus off us and puts that focus on others. When it comes to worship, thankfulness can help us get to a place where we can more fully place our eyes onto God in worship.

As we think about our worship, it's important to note that even though we don't worship our country, we still can be thankful for it, as well as for the freedoms we get to enjoy. For a Christian, patriotism is about worshiping God alone while being thankful for the country we get to enjoy. It's about seeing ourselves first as citizens of God's kingdom while being thankful citizens of our earthly country. It's impossible to seek God's kingdom without having a truly thankful heart for all that God has done for us.

DELIGHT

What are some of the commands listed in this psalm?

The psalmist encourages the people to worship in a number of ways in verses 1-4. What does the psalmist state as the reason for that worship in verse 5? Why is this so important?

What does it mean to acknowledge that the Lord is God?

DISPLAY

One of the biggest reasons we struggle with truly being thankful is the fast pace at which we tend to live our lives. Take some time to slow down today and be grateful. In the space below, create a list of all the things in your life you're thankful for. Start with practical things like having a place to live, food to eat, and air to breathe. Then move on to more eternal things, like salvation, new life in Christ, or the strength God gives you. Finally, before you move into your prayer time, think about a person whom you can talk with about the things you're thankful for.

Focus your prayer time today on gratitude. Take some time to thank God for the items on the list you created a moment ago. Thank Him for the gifts He gives us that we don't normally think about. Ask God to develop gratitude in your heart that will overflow into your worship and ultimately help you seek His kingdom in a new and deeper way.

DAY 10

FRIENDS OF GOD

READ JAMES 4:4-10.

You adulterous people! Don't you know that friendship with the world is hostility toward God? So whoever wants to be the friend of the world becomes the enemy of God.
— James 4:4

DISCOVER

It's easy to slip into what James calls "friendship with the world." We do this when we allow celebrity culture to be more important to us than God. We do it when we care more about what people think about us than what God thinks about us. We do this when we consume pop culture media like music or movies without reflecting on it. Many of us even do this with politics or love for our country. If our love for our country is greater than our love for God, then we cannot truly say we are friends of God.

Why does God care so much about our friendship with the world? Verse 5 describes it well for us. We belong to God alone when we come to faith in Jesus. His Spirit is jealous for our affection and attention. We can't put anything else as a higher priority—if we do, we are essentially claiming to have hatred and hostility toward God. Fortunately, God's grace gives us what we need to put Him as our priority and humbly seek Him above everything else.

DELIGHT

Why do you think these verses give such a strong warning about "friendship with the world" (v. 4)?

How does humbly seeking God and repenting of our sin help us develop a greater love for Him?

According to these verses, what type of person is God's grace given to? Why does God give grace to this type of person?

DISPLAY

In a world that seems to be constantly grabbing for your attention, how in the world do you make an effort at living out the truths in today's verses? First, it's important to recognize how the world can seek to befriend you. You may see this showing up in your life in different ways, such as entertainment, politics, or friendships. One way to determine any misplaced priorities you might have is to ask for help. Go to a Christian friend or leader whom you trust and ask that person to point out any areas where he or she sees you having greater friendship with the world than with God. Then, ask this person to help you take some next steps toward humbly seeking God first.

As you pray today, ask God to show you any areas of your life where you are displaying friendship with the world more than friendship with Him. Take your time and let Him show you blind spots that you might not have seen before. Repent of any areas that are holding you back from fully pursuing Christ as your greatest priority.

SECTION 2

YOUR KINGDO COM

Sometimes we are guilty of making "kingdoms" of things that will not last forever—things like our wealth, our social status, our looks, or even our nation. But the only kingdom that will endure is God's. Therefore, our desire should be for His kingdom to rule here on earth, just as it does in heaven. That is the only way for us to find peace in our lives and our world.

DAY 11

Kingdom Come

READ MATTHEW 6:9-15.

"Your kingdom come. Your will be done on earth as it is in heaven."
— Matthew 6:10

DISCOVER

A few years ago, something called the Ice Bucket Challenge became popular. The agenda for the ice bucket challenge was to raise awareness and money for research for ALS, a rare but fatal disease that causes people to gradually lose control of their muscles. The challenge became a viral trend that many people participated in and were excited about.

Have you ever gotten completely caught up in a trend and didn't realize it until you were in the middle of it? Some trends are worthy, like the ALS Ice Bucket Challenge, but some are not because they are attached to agendas that aren't aligned with the kingdom of God.

In the Lord's Prayer, Jesus isn't telling us that we need to pray these exact words (although we can!). Instead, He's giving us a template that includes the elements we should include in our prayers. Verse 10 emphasizes the importance of embracing God's kingdom agenda. When you hear "kingdom," you might think about a castle or an earthly ruler. But God's kingdom is His rule and reign over His people.

When we pray for God's kingdom to come, we are asking for God to rule and reign here on earth in the same way He rules and reigns in heaven. It's important to make sure we're caught up in the right agenda. As we grow older, we all face the temptation to embrace the agendas of political parties or other temporary perspectives of this world. Keep it a priority to make God's kingdom your priority.

DELIGHT

Which part of the Lord's Prayer is most meaningful to you? Why?

Notice how Jesus uses "us" in His prayer instead of "me." Why do you think that is?

Why is it important that the Lord's Prayer starts with recognizing who God is?

DISPLAY

Take some time to compare God's kingdom priorities with the world's kingdom priorities. Fill out the columns below, thinking of different values and priorities from each kingdom that are opposites of each other. For example, you might write "focused on others" in the list for God's kingdom and "self-centered" in the list for the world's kingdom. After you've listed a few items in each column, circle one or two priorities of God's kingdom that you'd like to pursue as a greater emphasis in your life.

GOD'S KINGDOM	WORLD'S KINGDOM

Use the Lord's Prayer as a model for your prayer time today. Start by acknowledging who God is and His holiness. Next, ask for His will to be done and submit your will to His. Ask Him to meet your needs as well as the needs of others. Repent and ask for forgiveness of any sins that come to mind. Finally, close your time by praying for His protection from temptation.

DAY 12

REAL LOVE

READ 1 CORINTHIANS 13:4-5.

Love is patient, love is kind. Love does not envy, is not boastful, is not arrogant, is not rude, is not self-seeking, is not irritable, and does not keep a record of wrongs.
— 1 Corinthians 13:4-5

DISCOVER

One of the marks of God's kingdom people is that they love others. In 1 Corinthians 13, we find the words of what is often called the "love chapter." But even though it's been read at many weddings over the years, it's not really a chapter about romantic relationships so much as it is a chapter about how the church is called to operate in love. In fact, the chapters both before and after chapter 13 relate to spiritual gifts and worship. Think about that. We throw around the word "love" a lot, but we don't always think about what it means. According to the Bible, it's connected to how we serve each other and worship God.

These verses help us clearly see how God defines love, and they show us how we are to love others as citizens of His kingdom. Love, according to the Bible, isn't primarily about a feeling—instead, it's defined by the way we treat other people. If we were to summarize love as it's defined in this chapter, we might say that biblical love is the action of seeking the best for other people in a way that honors God and honors those people. This type of love is much bigger than any emotion or feeling. We need to love others with biblical love if we want to be people who will see God's kingdom operating here on earth.

DELIGHT

How does 1 Corinthians 13 describe good works and spiritual actions that happen without love?

How do you see the love that's described in 1 Corinthians 13 lived out in our world today? Where do you see it missing?

Which description of love sounds the most challenging to live out?

DISPLAY

Re-read through this chapter again, but this time, every time you come across the word "love," use your name in its place. For example, "Ethan is patient, Ethan is kind . . ." As you read through the passage, notice the places where you pause for a second to think, "Hm, that's not really true about me." Pick one of those descriptions of love where you see yourself as lacking, and focus today on growing in that area you picked. Think of a practical way you can show love in that way that's been challenging to you in the past.

Focus your prayer time today on how you can grow in loving others the way God calls citizens of His kingdom to love. If there is a characteristic of love that's challenging for you, ask God to give you the strength to demonstrate that type of love. If there's a specific person you find difficult to love, ask God to give you the grace and strength to love him or her the way He does.

DAY 13

The Beauty of Tough Times

READ JAMES 1:2-4.

Consider it a great joy, my brothers and sisters,
whenever you experience various trials.
— James 1:2

DISCOVER

I'm willing to bet that you were a little surprised when you first read today's verses. Who in the world would consider it joy when going through tough times?! You're right that we shouldn't be thrilled about difficulties just because they're difficult. But put in proper perspective, you can find joy even when you go through tough times and trials. It's not the trial that brings you joy—it's what the trial produces.

Most pregnant mothers don't find joy in the pain of giving birth for its own sake. They find joy because they know that at the end of that pain is a baby to love and care for. Trials and tough times in your faith aren't always fun, but trials produce endurance in your life, and endurance is what produces maturity. That kind of spiritual maturity is something we should all be seeking as followers of Christ. And the reality is, we will all go through tough times because of our faith if we're serious about pursuing His kingdom.

DELIGHT

What are some types of trials Christians probably experienced when James wrote this letter two thousand years ago?

What are some types of trials followers of Christ experience today?

Why is it important to recognize the positive results that trials produce in our lives?

DISPLAY

I used to love Now & Later candies when I was a kid. What if you can think about the tough times in your life as being about both "now" and "later"? Start by picking a hard time you've gone through in your life and remember what it was like. At the time you were experiencing that hard time, it was "now." Then, think about what happened "later." How did God use that hard time?

Now, take a current area of your life that's difficult. Think about the challenge of it "now" and then what God may grow in you "later."

The reality for all of us is we've either just gone through a tough time, are in the middle of a tough time, or are getting ready to go through a tough time. Which one of those is you at the moment? Whichever it is, spend time in prayer today giving that tough time to God. If it's in the past, thank Him for bringing you through it. If it's now, ask Him for strength to endure. If you think it's still coming, ask Him to help you keep it in perspective when it arrives.

DAY 14

Be Courageous

READ JOHN 16:25-33.

"I have told you these things so that in me you may have peace. You will have suffering in this world. Be courageous! I have conquered the world."
— John 16:33

DISCOVER

One of the basic functions of government is to promote peace and protection—both from dangers in the communities we live in and from threats outside our borders. It's an essential task for those whom we've entrusted with leadership. However, even the peace our government can provide is limited. No earthly government can ever fully guarantee our peace or safety. This could sound a little scary if all your trust is in the government!

Fortunately, as Christians, we have a peace that's much bigger and better than what the government could ever offer. We are guaranteed to have hard times and to face suffering as followers of Jesus. The good news is we never face those times alone. He is always with us, and He already has conquered all that might cause us harm in the world. Our response is to courageously trust Jesus.

The encouragement and strength we have is because we now have direct access to the Father. Our faith in Jesus gives us full access to the Father and shows us how very much He loves us. We can rest in that truth.

DELIGHT

How does Jesus describe His relationship with the Father in these verses? Why is this important?

How did the disciples express their faith in Jesus in these verses? Is this similar to how you feel? Why or why not?

Why do you think Jesus told His disciples to be courageous even though they would all be scattered and He knew it?

DISPLAY

Where do you typically look to find peace? Is it in Jesus? Or do you seek out peace and comfort mainly from other things in this world? The life following Jesus is a constant journey of choosing against trusting in things other than God and shifting that trust to Him instead. We may find ourselves placing our trust in our own thoughts, our friends, or even the government. But God is calling us to choose to trust Him alone to bring us peace and security. Choose to find that peace in Him alone today. Think back over the last year. When has Jesus helped you find peace? Reflect on the questions below:

When has Jesus given you peace in the past week?

When has Jesus given you peace in the past month?

When has Jesus given you peace in the past year?

As you pray today, search your heart and ask God to show you areas where you've been trying to find peace apart from Him. Confess these areas to Him as He reveals them to you. Give them to Him and ask Him to replace them with a deep sense of trust in Him. Ask Him to give you the supernatural sense of peace that can only come from Him.

DAY 15

WAIT FOR THE LORD

READ PSALM 37.

Be silent before the LORD and wait expectantly for him; do not be agitated by one who prospers in his way, by the person who carries out evil plans.
— Psalm 37:7

DISCOVER

Patience is a virtue. Have you ever had someone tell you that? They probably said it to you at a time when you actually showed or felt impatience. We all want to be patient people, but it becomes difficult when life seems unfair. You're going about your business doing the right things and making good choices—then you see someone else making terrible decisions and choosing evil. The impatience kicks in when it seems like that person doesn't have to face any consequences at all. It seems like the person just gets away with it.

We live in a time where there is evil surrounding us all the time. Many people in our world choose to follow their own way instead of God's way—and it can be hard to deal with it when this happens. We might even be tempted to take matters into our own hands to make sure there are some consequences for these people. But if we're living for God's kingdom to come, we need to choose to patiently wait for God to take care of the situation. It's not our job to fix everything in the universe. There's only one God and none of us are Him. Waiting on His timing and trusting His judgment is always best.

DELIGHT

How does this psalm describe the person who chooses to live God's way? Is it hard for you to live this way? Why or why not?

How does this psalm encourage us to respond when it seems like evil is winning?

What promises does God give in this psalm? How do these promises bring you comfort?

DISPLAY

The problem with impatience is that it can lead to frustration, and this can lead us to hold grudges against people. Is there anyone in your life whom you're holding a grudge against or harboring bitterness and unforgiveness toward? The beauty of waiting for God to act on those who do evil is that it's a freeing experience. Holding on to impatience and frustration can destroy you. But the moment you choose patience and give it over to God is the moment you begin to experience freedom. Identify where you may have been choosing impatience or grudges with others, and begin the process of letting that go and simply leaving it in God's hands.

In your prayer time, confess to God where you've taken on the role of dealing out judgment and vengeance that's only meant for Him. Confess your impatience and the times when you rush to action. Submit yourself to God's control of our world, and ask Him to help you see situations through His eyes.

DAY 16

CONTRASTING ACTIONS

READ EPHESIANS 4:25-32.

*And be kind and compassionate to one another,
forgiving one another, just as God also forgave you in Christ.*
— Ephesians 4:32

DISCOVER

How do we know when God's kingdom is here on earth as it is in heaven? How do we know His will is being accomplished in that way? We can tell it's happening by the way God's people live and treat others.

Years ago, I heard a high school student make an interesting comment about another student she saw at a prayer rally at the school they both attended. She said, "I didn't even know he was a Christian." Now, it's possible that they might just not have been around each other much. But at the same time, it should be clear to others that you're a follower of Jesus because you're treating others with kindness, compassion, and forgiveness. Let's face it—those words don't describe the way most teenagers treat each other.

Today's verses are full of contrasts. We're told to avoid one behavior and pursue the opposite one. We're told not to speak one way but to speak a different way instead. The question for each of us is this: *Does my life reflect the kingdom of God to others?* If our answer to that question is no, it's time to pursue some change in our lives.

DELIGHT

What behaviors do these verses tell us to avoid? Why should we avoid them?

What behaviors do these verses tell us to put into action? Why are these good things to do?

What's the motivation for followers of Christ to forgive others? Why is forgiveness central to the Christian faith?

DISPLAY

The Christian life can seem really challenging if you feel like it's just about doing better in your own effort. You won't ever find enough energy through self-improvement to live the life God is calling you to. It has to be lived out through the power of the Holy Spirit and by the right motivations. A big way to stay motivated to be kind, compassionate, and forgiving to others is to keeping your focus on the forgiveness Jesus has shown you. We may want to treat people terribly through our own efforts, but those efforts will fail. We must continually remind ourselves of how God has forgiven us over and over. Today, reflect on how God has forgiven you and allow that to be the driving force behind how you treat and forgive others.

In your prayer time, take a moment to reflect on some of the negative behaviors listed in these verses, and ask God to reveal ones you may have been participating in. Ask Him to empower you to live out the opposite today. Submit your weak spots to Him as an opportunity to grow new patterns in your life.

"I HAVE TOLD YOU THESE THINGS

SO THAT IN ME YOU MAY HAVE

PEACE.

YOU WILL HAVE SUFFERING IN THIS WORLD.

BE COURAGEOUS!

I HAVE CONQUERED THE WORLD."

MEMORY VERSE – JOHN 16:33

DAY 17

SALT AND LIGHT

READ MATTHEW 5:13-16.

"In the same way, let your light shine before others, so that they may see your good works and give glory to your Father in heaven."
— Matthew 5:16

DISCOVER

Two things that were of great value in the ancient world of the Bible remain valuable today: salt and light. If you've ever seen a cooking show, you know the value of salt. Chefs regularly get critiqued by judges for not having enough seasoning—including salt—in their meals. The purpose of salt in these cases is to add flavor, which makes the dishes taste better.

When it comes to light, if you've ever been camping, you know its value. Trying to find a trail or meet up with friends once it gets dark is almost impossible without light. Light is necessary in dark places.

The Bible says that we are salt and light. Salt adds flavor, and light takes away darkness. Both of these elements are intended to make the world better. Salt that doesn't taste salty doesn't make sense, and neither does light that is dark. As followers of Jesus and citizens of His kingdom, we're to do what He has called us to do: be salt and light.

An interesting thing about salt is that when it's used correctly, it doesn't draw attention to itself—it draws attention to the food it's flavoring. In the same way, light doesn't draw attention to itself but to the object it's lighting. As we desire to see God's kingdom come on earth, we need to make sure we're not drawing attention primarily to ourselves. We're not the point. Instead, we're called to point people to God and His glory. Our outward actions are designed to showcase how great our God is.

DELIGHT

Why do you think Jesus used the ideas of salt and light to describe His followers?

Why might it be tempting sometimes for Christians to hide their light?

What are some good works that might cause others to give glory to your Father in heaven?

DISPLAY

Light usually works best when it's used intentionally. Create a list of five people you know—perhaps friends, family members, neighbors, or teammates—who need to come to know Jesus as their Savior. Next to each name, write down one way you can intentionally shine the light of Jesus into that person's life. It might be a simple act of service followed by a few words about Jesus, or maybe it could be an encouraging note with a Scripture verse included. It might even just be grabbing some food with a that person and asking some questions about her or his spiritual life.

As you pray, mention the list of people you wrote down who need to know Jesus. Take time to pray for each one and his or her individual situation. Ask God to give you opportunities for gospel conversations with these people. Ask Him to give you courage and strength to step into those opportunities as they arise.

DAY 18

TWO MASTERS

READ LUKE 16:10-13.

"Whoever is faithful in very little is also faithful in much, and whoever is unrighteous in very little is also unrighteous in much."
— Luke 16:10

DISCOVER

What have you done with what you've been given? The reality is that God has given each of us different gifts, skills, and circumstances. You have talents and abilities that are different than your friends' talents and abilities. You may have financial resources that someone else doesn't have. We've all been given something even if we don't realize it. What are you doing with what you've been given?

Jesus pointed out the reality that if we have very little but we do something with it, then we will end up doing the same when we're blessed with a lot. But if we waste away the little we have, we'll end up doing the same when we get more.

Everything we have comes from God. But we'll run into trouble if our attention is torn between trying to serve God as our master and trying to serve someone else the same way. The same principle applies to God's kingdom versus the kingdom of this world. We can't live for both God's agenda and our country's agenda at the same time. We can't live for God's agenda and our own selfish agenda. We have to decide that God alone will be our master.

DELIGHT

How do you think Jesus's original hearers might have responded to this teaching?

What are some resources and gifts that God gives to believers?

Why is it impossible to serve two masters?

DISPLAY

Reflect on some areas where you might be tempted to divide your attention between God and something else. There can be all sorts of areas in our lives that try to be our "master." Now, it's important to realize serving God alone doesn't mean that you drop out of school, quit your sports team or band, and just sit in your room reading the Bible all day. It means that you have a clear vision in your mind of who your true master is and how that affects the other areas of your life. Take some time to adjust any of your priorities that need to be adjusted. Name one area of your life where you have struggled to make Jesus your master. Spend some time praying about this and give it to God.

As you pray, focus the first part of your prayer as a time of worship. Praise God for who He is as the One in charge of your life. Thank Him for the gifts He has given you. Worship Him because He is worthy of all your praise. Take the last part of your prayer time to submit your priorities to God and allow Him to be in charge and the master of all that you are.

DAY 19

A GENTLE RESPONSE

READ 1 PETER 3:13-17.

Yet do this with gentleness and reverence, keeping a clear conscience, so that when you are accused, those who disparage your good conduct in Christ will be put to shame.
— 1 Peter 3:16

DISCOVER

You are eventually going to be attacked for your faith if you're living a life for God's kingdom. There will be a day when people will see the difference in your life and will try to figure out what's different about you—and they may not come to positive conclusions. You'll need to be ready to give a defense for your faith. When that moment comes, you'll have a choice in how you give that defense. Will you show up with a hostile attitude or will you demonstrate gentleness and reverence?

One of the challenges when we defend our faith is deciding if we're truly concerned with sharing the gospel or if we're more concerned with just being right. If we're most concerned about sharing the gospel, we'll approach the other person with kindness. But if our main goal is to prove that we're right, we're probably going to end up in an argument and end up doing damage to both our witness and the cause of Christ.

To see His kingdom come here on earth as it is in heaven, we have to live like heaven is already here on earth, even though it's not. How we will treat each other then is how we must treat each other now. Being gentle and respectful—even to those who belittle you, insult you, or try to hurt you with their words—might be challenging, but it's how we conduct ourselves in a way that doesn't put Jesus to shame.

DELIGHT

What does it mean to suffer for righteousness?

How did Jesus suffer for His righteousness?

Who gets put to shame in this passage if we keep a clear conscience? Why is this important?

DISPLAY

There are plenty of opportunities for Christians in the United States to be looked down on for our faith. It's not popular to stand strong on the truths of the Bible. This means you must understand that often, your faith won't make you the most popular person around. At the same time, we shouldn't give reasons for people who aren't following Jesus to look down on us. Commit yourself to living a life that honors Christ and to treating others the way He has called you to treat them. If you do, when attacks come, your opponents won't have any extra ammunition to sling your way.

As you spend time in prayer today, ask God to give you a spirit of gentleness and reverence as you defend your faith. Confess any times when you've been rude or cruel to non-believers. Ask God to give you the strength to respond appropriately to any negativity you may face for your faith.

DAY 20

STAY ALERT

READ 1 PETER 4:7-11.

The end of all things is near; therefore, be alert and sober-minded for prayer.
— 1 Peter 4:7

DISCOVER

No one knows exactly when Jesus will return. But we do know that we are closer to that moment today than Peter was when he wrote this letter. Your teenage years are a season when it's easy to think you'll just go on living life forever as it is right now. But we each have a choice: we can fill our days with things that won't matter beyond our lives, or we can spend time investing in things that will last for eternity.

Our focus should be one of self-control as we are alert and sober-minded. It's about being intentional in your life as you follow Jesus. You will never become a mature disciple if you just "let it happen." You must make the decision to engage in the life God has called you to live and be disciplined in pursuing it. How do you want to be found when Jesus returns? You can either be floating through life without purpose or intentionally engaged in the pursuit of knowing Jesus and helping others know Him. That is what it means to live for His kingdom to come here on earth.

DELIGHT

What are some of the simple commands Peter gives us in these verses? Why do you think they are simple?

What do you think it looks like to be alert and sober-minded?

Why is it important for us to focus on serving others?

DISPLAY

One of the main ideas in these verses is that God has given you at least one spiritual gift. Imagine for a moment that you received the perfect present for Christmas . . . but then you never used the gift after opening it. That would be crazy, right? Well, God gave you spiritual gifts to use them serving others. It's okay if you're not sure what your gifts are. Take some time this week to serve in an area of your church. Afterward, reflect on whether or not it came easily to you, seemed to impact other people, or gave you joy. If so, maybe you're on the path to figuring out one of your spiritual gifts.

The first verse in our Scripture today has an emphasis on being sober-minded for prayer. As you pray today, engage in the time with a serious spirit. Don't go fast as you pray—take your time to reflect on all that God may want you to pray about. Slow down and listen to Him. Be alert to what He may be saying.

HOW TO
AS STRAN
AND EX

SECTION 3

LIVE
GERS
ILES

The truth is, no matter what country you live in or where you're originally from, if you've placed your faith in Jesus, this world is not your home. As followers of Jesus, we are citizens of God's kingdom, and we are called to live in such a way that the world around us sees that we belong to a place not of this world.

DAY 21

STRANGERS

READ 1 PETER 2:11-12.

Dear friends, I urge you as strangers and exiles to abstain from sinful desires that wage war against the soul.
— 1 Peter 2:11

DISCOVER

Think for a moment about what makes your home feel like home. It's most likely a combination of the people, the furniture, and maybe even the familiar smells. Home should be the place we feel most comfortable. As followers of Jesus, our true home is in heaven—yet we often find ourselves getting very comfortable in this world. Imagine if you could instead see yourself as described in these verses—as a stranger and exile in this world. It's not your home!

All of us can agree that we have sinful desires that wage war against our souls. We each face temptation every day. Part of the process of holding back from those desires is examining how you view yourself. If you see yourself as a citizen of this world, you're going to want to live like the people of this world. But if you see yourself as a stranger and exile—and recognize that your real home is in heaven—you're going to be able to see these sinful desires as foreign and unnatural to the place you truly belong. This second viewpoint will help you embrace the values of your heavenly home instead of this earthly foreign country where you happen to live for the time being.

DELIGHT

How do people who are "strangers and exiles" (v. 11) behave in places that are not their home? Do any of these behaviors reflect how we should live as followers of Jesus? How so?

What are some temptations that you frequently find yourself fighting against?

What's the ultimate goal of living differently in this world, according to verse 12?

DISPLAY

Imagine that you moved to a foreign country for a year. You'd feel uncomfortable in many ways. Other people might feel uncomfortable around you, too. But there's one important thing to remember: you would be the main example people have of what someone from your home country is like. Hopefully, you'd represent your home country well. As a foreigner in this world, keep in mind that you're the picture of what your true home—God's kingdom—is like. Reflect on what kind of picture you're presenting to the world. Below, write out one area where you are a good example of your true home and one area where you can grow and be a better witness for the kingdom of God.

Use today's prayer time to confess times when sinful desires have won the battle in your heart. Search your heart for any areas of sin that you've been hanging onto and confess them to God. Ask Him to forgive and to help you live in the ways of His kingdom going forward. Ask God to help you see yourself as a temporary resident of this world we live in.

DAY 22

HONORING AUTHORITY

READ 1 PETER 2:13-17.

Honor everyone. Love the brothers and sisters.
Fear God. Honor the emperor.
— 1 Peter 2:17

DISCOVER

As a follower of Jesus, you're called to submit to the human authorities God has placed in your life. It's interesting that Peter says we're to do this "because of the Lord" (v. 13). You probably don't often think about obeying authorities as being a spiritual issue; it likely just seems like something we have to do in life. But God has placed authorities in our lives for our own good. Laws and governments exist to protect us and to promote good in society.

Can you imagine what it would be like if there were no rules for how to drive a car? People would be driving at whatever speed they want and on the wrong side of the road, maybe bouncing off other cars as they went. Authority has a good place in our society because it was designed by God. We obey authority in our lives because God commanded it, and if we live as law-abiding citizens, that gives one less opportunity for people who might be against our faith to be critical of us. We need to be careful not to create reasons for people to find wrongdoing in us. Submission to authority helps guard against that.

DELIGHT

How do these verses change or strengthen your view of authorities in your life, like police officers, teachers, or coaches?

What would be an example of a time when it's okay to disobey authority, according to Scripture?

How does this passage seem to instruct us to see the idea of freedom in our lives?

DISPLAY

List out all the different authorities in your life that you can think of, (including those at home, at school, and in your community). You can list both general authorities like "police officers" as well as specific ones, like "my chemistry teacher." Next to each name, write down one way you currently submit to that authority, one thing that challenges you sometimes about her or his authority, and one way you can grow in your submission to that authority figure.

Focus your prayer time on the authorities in your life. Pray for wisdom and direction for government officials. Pray for teachers and administrators at your school. Pray for your parents. Pray for the spiritual leaders in your church. Ask God to give you strength with authorities whom you struggle to submit to.

DAY 23

SUBMISSION TO AUTHORITY

READ ROMANS 13:1-7.

Let everyone submit to the governing authorities,
since there is no authority except from God,
and the authorities that exist are instituted by God.
— Romans 13:1

DISCOVER

Today we're going to dive a little deeper into this idea of authority. In Romans 13, Paul writes about submitting to governing authorities, just like Peter did in the verses we looked at yesterday. But Paul gives a little more explanation of where authority comes from. All authority comes from God—He is the One who puts governing authorities in place. When governments function the way they are meant to, they are God's tools to bring about justice in our society. When they do not, they must ultimately answer to God, just like all people do.

When we recognize that every authority figure has been put into place by God, it can completely flip the way we think about authority in our lives. It changes how we view disobedience because now, we're not just disobeying that teacher, police officer, or parent—we're disobeying God Himself.

We honor God when we submit to the authorities He has put in place in our lives. We might think getting in trouble on earth is the worst that happens when we disobey authorities, but it's really not. When we disobey authorities who lead us to good and right actions, we're ultimately disobeying God in heaven. We must choose instead to trust governing authorities with the responsibility that God entrusted to them, as long as they are not leading us to actions or activities that are contrary to God's design and desires.

DELIGHT

How can someone make sure to not be afraid of authority but to pay it the proper respect it requires?

How does it change your view of authority to realize it comes from God?

What are some ways we can honor God by honoring the authority figures in our lives?

DISPLAY

Imagine if God hadn't put authority figures in place to lead us here on earth. What would society be like if murderers were never punished? What would our country be like if people could steal and get away with it? How would your city or town suffer if people did whatever they wanted to? Sometimes when we imagine what life would be like without something, it helps us appreciate that thing even more. Think about the reasons you're grateful for the authorities whom God has placed in your life. Be grateful that He loves us enough to provide boundaries for us to live by. In the space below, list three boundaries that you are grateful for. Then list a boundary that you are tempted to push, and ask God to help you submit to His authority in your life in that area.

Use your prayer time as an opportunity for confession. There may be authority figures in your life whom you haven't been fully submitting to. Ask God to show you the gaps in your obedience to authority. Confess to Him how you haven't honored or obeyed Him when you've chosen to go your own way against authority.

DAY 24

Obeying Leaders

READ HEBREWS 13:10-19.

For we do not have an enduring city here;
instead, we seek the one to come.
— Hebrews 13:14

DISCOVER

God has placed authority in our lives for our own good. But there are times when the governing authorities go too far and break away from God's Word. For example, in Daniel 3:4-6, the law commanded that everyone bow down in worship to the king. This stood directly against God's command to worship no one other than Him, so the Hebrew exiles, Shadrach, Meshach, and Abednego, rightly refused to obey this law.

For the most part, we should make every effort to obey authorities in our lives. Hebrews 13:14 gives us a great principle to help guide our thinking on when not to obey governing authorities. The culture and society we live in currently won't last forever—no earthly government is permanent. We should always look ahead to be part of the heavenly city, which will last forever.

As followers of Jesus, we are citizens of two kingdoms: we have responsibilities to the current, temporary kingdom and to the authorities God has placed over us while we live here. At the same time, we have a responsibility to the kingdom of God. We must make sure we don't get too comfortable living in the kingdom that won't last. Laws that require us to sin against God are laws we should not obey. Ultimately, we will answer to God alone, and the leaders of our earthly governments will answer to Him as well.

DELIGHT

Re-read verse 15. What does it mean to offer a sacrifice of praise?

What reasons do these verses give for obeying our leaders?

DISPLAY

We are called to obey government authorities unless they require us to sin. List some potential actions a government could ask someone to do that would be sin and the Scripture verses each action would go against. It's possible these could be individual actions or even actions required of a group, such as a church. Next to each, write down what a potential consequence could be for not following the direction of the government. Write down how you might respond instead of following the sinful direction. What will you do if you face this type of decision in your life? Decide now that you will always make obeying God your first response.

Ask God for wisdom and discernment as you go through life. Ask Him to help you see clearly when governing authorities may be asking a follower of Jesus to do something contrary to God's design and desires. Commit yourself to choosing God's way instead of the world's way, no matter the consequences.

DAY 25

GIVE IT TO GOD

READ MATTHEW 22:15-22.

Then he said to them, "Give, then, to Caesar the things that are Caesar's, and to God the things that are God's."
— Matthew 22:21

DISCOVER

By now, you most likely get the point: God calls us to respect, honor, and obey the authorities and governments that God has placed in our lives. In our verses today, the Pharisees tried to trick Jesus, as they often did. They hoped they could stir Jesus up to either speak too lowly of God (so that He could be accused of blasphemy) or to speak poorly of the Roman government (so that He could be accused of treason). Instead, Jesus surprised them by asking a question showing that He saw right through their trick, as He often did.

One way to look at these verses is to simply see it as commanding people to pay their taxes. But think about the idea of giving to God the things that are God's. God desires your entire life. Yes, you have obligations to the government, but they are small in comparison to your obligations to God. We should respect authorities, but we should honor and respect God above all. All things belong to Him.

DELIGHT

Why do you think the Pharisees were trying to trick Jesus?

How did Jesus respond to their question? How do you think you would have responded in a similar situation?

Why do you think the Pharisees were amazed with Jesus's response?

DISPLAY

You're probably not paying much (if anything) in taxes at this time in your life. So, you might wonder if this passage really applies to you at all right now. One other thing this passage shows us is that there is a time and place for being a good citizen of your country. It's good to pledge allegiance to the American flag and to sing the National Anthem. It's good to vote and be involved in the process of government. But always keep in mind that the best pursuit in your life is to put God above everything else. What is one way you can put God above everything else today?

Take time as you pray today to thank God for the things He provides through the different levels of government in your life. God provides good gifts and He can even do so through normal things like schools, roads, and parks. Ask Him to give you the right perspective when it comes to knowing what belongs to the authority of government and what belongs to God.

DAY 26

A DIFFERENT KINGDOM

READ JOHN 18:28-38.

"My kingdom is not of this world," said Jesus. "If my kingdom were of this world, my servants would fight, so that I wouldn't be handed over to the Jews. But as it is, my kingdom is not from here."
— John 18:36

DISCOVER

The Jewish people in the first century didn't love the fact that their land was occupied and governed by Rome. They had been conquered many times before in their history, and now they were again under the authority of another nation. They were looking for a Messiah, a Chosen One, to lead them to freedom. The problem was, they had all sorts of expectations about what this Messiah should be like. Some thought He would be a political leader and would take control from Rome through political means. Others thought He would be a military leader and would overthrow the Roman government by force.

But as Jesus responded to Pilate, the Roman governor, it became clear that He was not the type of Messiah people had been looking for. Pilate questioned Jesus about what He had done, and Jesus responded by pointing out that His followers hadn't resisted His arrest with violence or sought to free Him through force. Why? Because Jesus's kingdom is different. His kingdom isn't one of violence but one of turning the other cheek. His kingdom is truly not of this world, and it operates differently than the way this world operates.

DELIGHT

What do you think Pilate was trying to get the Pharisees to admit? What was he asking of Jesus through his conversation with Him?

What do you think it means that Jesus's kingdom is "not of this world" (v. 36)?

In verse 37, what does Jesus say His purpose was for coming into the world? Why is this important?

DISPLAY

It's easy to fall into the habit of doing things a certain way just because that's what everyone else does. The world looks down on people whom it sees as "less than." The world strives to get ahead, no matter the cost. The world justifies hidden behavior if that behavior doesn't seem to hurt anyone else. But Jesus calls us to be part of a different type of kingdom, one that responds to the world in a different way. Create a list of some ways His kingdom operates differently than the world's kingdom. Seek to pursue His kingdom priorities rather than the world's.

In your prayer time, ask God to show you areas of your life where you may have slid into operating in the same way as the world. Ask Him to reveal areas where you don't look very different from the world. Submit those areas to Him and ask for His strength to live differently. Commit yourself to following the ways of His kingdom instead of the ways of the world.

MEMORY VERSES

OUR CITIZENSHIP IS IN HEAVEN,
AND WE EAGERLY WAIT
FOR A SAVIOR FROM THERE,
THE LORD JESUS CHRIST.
HE WILL TRANSFORM THE BODY
OF OUR HUMBLE CONDITION
INTO THE LIKENESS OF HIS
GLORIOUS BODY,
BY THE POWER THAT ENABLES HIM
TO SUBJECT EVERYTHING
TO HIMSELF.
— PHILIPPIANS 3:20-21

DAY 27

Praying for Authority

READ 1 TIMOTHY 2:1-7.

First of all, then, I urge that petitions, prayers, intercessions, and thanksgivings be made for everyone, for kings and all those who are in authority, so that we may lead a tranquil and quiet life in all godliness and dignity.
— 1 Timothy 2:1-2

DISCOVER

Whom do you typically pray for? Maybe you pray for your family and friends. You probably pray for things for yourself sometimes. You might even pray for your teachers to go easy on grading that test you just took. But when was the last time you prayed for the people leading our government? It's probably not the first thing that comes to mind. In today's verses, Paul reminds his young pastor friend Timothy about the importance of this very thing.

The reason Paul gives for praying for government officials is pretty simple. It's so we can live a simple life that's devoted to godliness. It works out to our benefit when the government is able to keep the peace and we're able to simply follow Jesus. Ultimately, this helps us to be able to share the good news of Jesus with more people. You might not think that praying for the government has a spiritual impact on people in our country, but it absolutely does.

DELIGHT

What are the four types of prayers that Paul describes in verse 1? How are they different from each other?

According to these verses, what is the only way for us to reach God? Why does this matter?

What is God's desire for all people? How can you help others know this truth?

DISPLAY

Create a prayer list so that you can pray for different people in government every day of the week. Don't just pray for specific positions (like "mayor")—pray for the people who are serving in these positions by name. Here are some suggestions of people you can look up to add to your list: city council members, your city's mayor, your state legislature officials, your congressperson, your senators, the vice president, and the president. You could even pray for members of the United States Supreme Court. Even if you don't agree with everything these people stand for—and even if you don't like them!—you can still choose to pray for them every day.

It's time to put this into practice. Pick someone in a government position, and use your time today to pray for that person specifically. Pray for his or her health. Ask God to bless his or her family. Pray that this person will make wise decisions. Pray that the person would grow in his or her relationship with Jesus or come to know Jesus for the first time.

DAY 28

WHO'S GETTING YOUR BEST?

READ MALACHI 1:6-14.

"When you present a blind animal for sacrifice, is it not wrong? And when you present a lame or sick animal, is it not wrong? Bring it to your governor! Would he be pleased with you or show you favor?" asks the LORD of Armies.
— Malachi 1:8

DISCOVER

The United States is a country that loves excellence. We want to do our best and pride ourselves on being the greatest. Our country has a rich history of brilliant innovation, sacrificial service, and hard work. But are we willing to give our best to our country and only our leftovers to God?

The prophet Malachi brought a challenging message to God's people in his day. The Old Testament law required that people bring the best animals from their flocks for sacrifice. Yet people would bring the animals they didn't care about losing and keep the best ones for themselves. This was a huge offense to God!

Can you imagine God asking you for your best and you only giving Him the leftovers? God has blessed you with talents, resources, and abilities. He calls you to give your absolute best of those gifts. He wants you to see Him as worthy of your best. Maybe that's the problem. It just may be that we see God as an optional part of our lives, one who isn't really worthy of our best. If we view God as just a leftover in our schedule, we'll never be at a place where we desire to give Him our best in worship, service, and everything.

DELIGHT

Whom was Malachi speaking to in these verses? Why is this important?

What was the Lord's main argument against Israel?

What does the last verse in our reading for today mean for us right now in our daily lives?

DISPLAY

Think about where you may be offering God leftovers in your life. Is He not getting your full attention when you read the Bible? Are you practicing true generosity with your money? Do you only go to church services when it's convenient for you? Our lives are full of so many things that we can often push God to the side and simply give Him leftovers instead of our best. Choose to give Him your best going forward. Start by choosing to give Him the best part of your attention today, when you're most alert, to spend time with Him.

To give God our best, we need to make sure we have an accurate view of Him. Spend time in prayer today focused on the greatness of God. Praise Him for His faithfulness. Worship Him for His creativity. Thank Him for His grace and mercy. Submit yourself to offering Him your best instead of merely your leftovers.

DAY 29

NO SEPARATION

READ ROMANS 8:31-39.

For I am persuaded that neither death nor life, nor angels nor rulers, nor things present nor things to come, nor powers, nor height nor depth, nor any other created thing will be able to separate us from the love of God that is in Christ Jesus our Lord.
— Romans 8:38-39

DISCOVER

Have you ever gotten separated from your parents? It can be pretty scary. I grew up in Southern California a few hours away from Disneyland. Every time we'd go to the park, we'd do the same thing right when we walked in: my mom would point out the place we were supposed to meet if we were separated at any point during the day. We had a solid plan in case I was too distracted by all the fun!

But it's scary to think about being separated from those you love. When it comes to your relationship with Jesus, you might worry that He will leave you or you'll somehow ended up separated from Him. Here's some good news: NOTHING can ever separate us from God's love. Nothing on this earth—whether it's physical, spiritual, or even the laws where we live—can separate from the love we have in Jesus. You don't have to worry.

DELIGHT

After reading these verses today, how do you think we should respond when we feel accused or condemned?

What do you think it means to be "more than conquerors" (v. 37)?

How does it make you feel to realize that God is for you, not against you? What changes does this inspire you to make in your life?

DISPLAY

Take some time to journal about how it makes you feel to know that nothing can separate you from God's love. You might want to focus on some specific aspects that are mentioned in the passage. Or you might focus on doubts you've had about God's love for you and how these verses answer those doubts. You could even zero in on how you can help a friend gain a greater understanding of God's love for her or him in spite of what that friend might expect His love to be.

Spend your time in prayer as a moment of gratitude for God's love for you. Since He has loved you in such an incredible way, express your love to Him through your prayer. Thank Him for loving you when you were unlovable. Thank Him for not allowing anything to separate you from His love. Ask Him to help you keep His love as the focus of your mind throughout the day.

DAY 30

TRUE CITIZENSHIP

READ PHILIPPIANS 3:12-21.

Our citizenship is in heaven, and we eagerly wait for a Savior from there, the Lord Jesus Christ. He will transform the body of our humble condition into the likeness of his glorious body, by the power that enables him to subject everything to himself.
— Philippians 3:20-21

DISCOVER

When I was a kid, my school gave out citizenship awards. Maybe yours does something like that too. At my school, this was basically an award you'd get if you were nice to other students, helped out the teacher, or picked up other people's trash after lunch—in other words, if you were a good citizen of the school.

It's a good thing to train kids to be good citizens and it's a good thing to try to be good citizens as we continue getting older. But sometimes we can get confused and think life is all about just being a good citizen in our city, our country, or on our planet. While that's important, God calls us to a life that is so much more!

We need to recognize where our true citizenship is. As Christians, we all have dual citizenship—we're citizens of heaven and we're citizens here on earth. But we must recognize that our true and most important citizenship is in heaven. That's where we need to keep our eyes. This life is not all there is—we'll spend much more time in heaven than we will here on earth. So, let's look forward to our true citizenship in heaven as we live out our temporary citizenship here on earth.

DELIGHT

Why is it important to forget what is behind and reach forward to what's ahead?

Why is it important to have role models in the faith whom we can imitate?

How can you keep your focus on being a citizen of heaven?

DISPLAY

Under each label below, list thoughts, actions, and attitudes that would fall under each category. Try to come up with at least five or six on each list. Now, look at the lists you just created. Where would you say the majority of your attention is focused? If most of your attention is on being a citizen of earth, think of a couple of ways you can devote more attention to being a citizen of heaven. If most of your attention is on being a citizen of heaven, think of a few people with whom you can share the gospel soon so they might one day be citizens of heaven as well.

HEAVEN-FOCUSED	EARTH-FOCUSED

Express your heart to God in prayer as you eagerly wait for Jesus. Share your frustrations about the current state of the world with God. Share with Him about the challenges you're facing in your daily life. Ask Him to give you eyes to look beyond this present world. Ask Him to help you pursue a greater desire to live for what lasts forever. Commit your heart to being a citizen of heaven.

RIGHT, WRONG, OR ILLEGAL?

Let's play a quick game about laws. Circle True or False for each one below.

True or False	1. In San Diego, it's illegal to display your Christmas lights after February 2.
True or False	2. Florida declared it illegal to start a rumor on Christmas Day.
True or False	3. If it's a Sunday in New York, it's illegal to put an ice cream cone in your back pocket.
True or False	4. You can't plow a cotton field with an elephant if you live in North Carolina.
True or False	5. It's illegal to groom your cat with a hairbrush made for humans in South Dakota.

(See the bottom of page 111 for answers.)

Does it surprise you to know that some of these are real laws? They might seem a little weird, but each of them was created for a reason.

1. The law about Christmas lights in San Diego was created for both personal safety and to reduce light pollution. After ninety days, these twinkling outdoor lights get weathered and can cause significant electrical issues.[1]

3. Though no one knows for sure, the law about ice cream cones likely comes from a set of religious laws about what you can and can't do on Sunday. It's assumed that people would put the offending ice cream cones in their pockets to avoid getting tickets.[2]

4. The origins of this law are mostly unconfirmed, but it's assumed that this dates back to P. T. Barnum's misuse of both elephants and North Carolina farmland as a marketing ploy for his circus.[3]

Sometimes the reasons behind laws fall within common sense, but sometimes they have a darker past or darker application. Consider how laws concerning religion have been misused over the years—even Jesus spoke against ridiculous rules being added to God's commands, since God doesn't need us to add anything to His perfect Word. Consider how the plowing of fields with elephants could have harmed the animals, the land, and even the crop production and profits of the farmers.

These started as "silly" examples, but when we dig deep, even most of them have a darker past. Yes, mostly laws are meant to protect us. But the truth is, some things are perfectly legal yet still wrong. Throughout history, there have been people who spoke up against terrible wrongs knowing they might face incredible consequences for doing so.

Read Exodus 1:15-22. Describe the command Pharaoh gave, how the women responded, and what happened to them as a result.

Far worse than being bullied for beliefs, over six million Jews—along with millions of others—were killed between 1933 and 1945 in the Holocaust.[4] The Nazis believed that Germans were superior and that Jews posed a threat to their race. But many people stood against the Nazis' rules, and the actions of these brave individuals spoke volumes.

Look up information about the Dutch woman Corrie ten Boom. Describe describe what she did to stand against the Nazis' rules.

Choose one of the following people. Do some research about your chosen person, and on a separate piece of paper, write some notes about his or her work in abolishing slavery. Make sure to discuss the consequences this person faced, both good and bad, for his or her bold stance.

Frederick Douglass
William Lloyd Garrison
Harriet Beecher Stowe
Sojourner Truth
Harriet Tubman
Hannah More
William Wilberforce
Angelina Grimké

While Scripture says we should follow the laws of our earthly governments, it specifies that we can disobey when those laws go against God's law, God's heart, or God's desires. You might not ever have to choose between doing the right thing in God's eyes and the legal thing in your government's eyes, but you might face rejection or exclusion or take a hit to your social status.

Take a look at the following list. Circle things that are wrong and put an X through anything that's illegal.

- Bullying
- Speeding
- Jaywalking
- Pornography
- Lying
- Sex before marriage
- Sharing streaming account passwords
- Littering
- Gossip
- Texting and driving
- Being rude
- Downloading music without paying
- Copying your friend's homework

Some of the "wrong" things on the list above are specifically named in the Bible, while some we know to be wrong because of other truths in God's Word. For example, pornography as we know it wasn't an issue in Jesus's day, but the Bible talks about sexual immorality and crude talk being wrong (see 1 Cor. 6:18; Eph. 5:4).

What else comes to mind as being wrong or not God-honoring but isn't against the law?

Let's look at a few scenarios. Determine how you would respond to each one and why.

A group at your school has been bullying a friend of yours because of his cultural heritage.

In gym class, a dodgeball team captain refuses to pick anyone who was born outside the United States.

Many people ignore the autistic student in your class, despite his desire for friendship.

Again, you may never have to step in to help others in scenarios like these. But one day, you will have to choose whether to speak up about something or stay silent. Every day, you have to choose God's way over the world's way, right over wrong—regardless of the consequences.

The good news is that God is with you as you stand. God is with you as you speak up. God is with you as you face what comes after. And many times, God will uniquely bless you when you seek what honors Him above all else.

Answers from page 108: 1. True; 2. False; 3. True; 4. True; 5. False

Sources:

1. "What's Bugging You? Christmas lights up after the holidays," ABC7, February 8, 2012, https://abc7.com/archive/8536507/.

2. James Loren, "10 Strange New York City Laws," Goldberg and Loren, June 20, 2023, https://goldbergloren.com/10-strange-new-york-city-laws.

3. Katie Quine, "What's With North Carolina's Weird Laws?" Our State, March 9, 2015, https://www.ourstate.com/north-carolina-weird-laws/.

4. "How Many People Did the Nazis Murder?" Holocaust Encyclopedia, United States Holocaust Memorial Museum, last edited September 26, 2023, https://encyclopedia.ushmm.org/content/en/article/documenting-numbers-of-victims-of-the-holocaust-and-nazi-persecution.

LIFEWAY STUDENT DEVOTIONS

Engage with God's Word.

lifeway.com/teendevotionals

- [ ] WITH YOU

- [ ] ROMANS

- [ ] LOVE AND JUSTICE

- [ ] CALLED TO THIS

- [ ] GROWING IN GRATITUDE

- [ ] GOD WITH US

- [ ] MADE NEW

- [ ] LOVE WITH ALL YOUR HEART

- [ ] RISEN

- [ ] WISDOM, STATURE, AND FAVOR

- [ ] BEFORE YOU GO

- [ ] PRESS PAUSE